HOW TO CLOSE YOUR ESTATE WITH EASE

By

Janise L. Bradford

authorHOUSE

1663 LIBERTY DRIVE, SUITE 200
BLOOMINGTON, INDIANA 47403
(800) 839-8640
www.authorhouse.com

First published by AuthorHouse 04/28/05

ISBN: 1-4184-1074-8 (e)
ISBN: 1-4184-1075-6 (sc)
ISBN: 1-4208-5249-3 (dj)

Printed in the United States of America
Bloomington, IN

This book is printed on acid-free paper.

DEDICATION

I give all praise and glory to God almighty through my Lord and Savior Jesus Christ for being there, and loving me at all times. I thank you Lord, for giving me the heart, strength, courage, and endurance to keep going. We can surely do all things through Christ, who gives us strength.

I dedicate this book to my late father, Lewis L. Winchester, Sr. who taught me by his example that honesty, determination, and hard work are three sure ingredients for success. His truth and light shall live on in my heart forever.

Lastly, with the utmost love, admiration, and respect, I thank my husband, Aaron. Having you in my life is evidence that dreams really do come true. Thank you for your unconditional love, encouragement, and support.

TABLE OF CONTENTS

INTRODUCTION

How to Close Your Estate with Ease is a simple approach that has been designed to provide detailed information for you to consider so that you can make very intelligent, well informed decisions which will enable you to communicate more effectively with your attorney and other professional advisors when going through the process of closing an estate.

Being a hands-on personal representative will provide much better protection for the estate for which you have been appointed to represent.

If you learn more about how the probate process works, you will no doubt be able to communicate more effectively with your attorney which would in turn result in less billable hours by your attorney. Here, you will receive a step by step overview of how to close an estate. After being equipped with the knowledge contained here, you will quickly discover just how non-intimidating the probate process actually is. Follow the steps in this book and you will soon have the knowledge to efficiently assist with closing any simple estate with complete confidence.

It is important to note that the information contained here is not designed to take the place of an attorney. In fact, in some states, having an attorney to close estates is required by law.

Also, in some states there are simple forms available for you to do it yourself, by simply completing 'do it yourself' forms provided by the court. You will need to check with your local probate court to inquire as to whether your particular state has a self service center and to help you determine exactly what your state requirements are for probating estates under those particular guidelines.

Normally, the personal representative will do no more than sign documents as directed by the attorney of record. While there will be many documents that will need to be signed by you and subsequently filed with the court by your attorney, there is still a great deal that you can do throughout this process that could equate to a worthwhile savings to the estate. The process is not difficult, and basically, aside from the knowledge contained here, all you will need is time, and some very basic organizational skills. By following the steps contained in this book, you may only need an attorney for actual court filings, and formal communications among heirs (if it should become necessary to do so), and other court matters that should arise.

Try to negotiate a fee with the attorney that you are both comfortable with since you will be doing much of the work. In this case, instead of paying a flat fee, you may wish to pay by the hour since you will be trimming many hours off by doing a great deal of the work yourself. Not only will you be saving money for the estate, but you will also be saving the attorney a lot of time and effort.

As stated above, for the most part, the attorney in essence would be filing all of your court documents as well as providing you with legal advice. In some cases it may be necessary for your attorney to represent the estate in some type of actual court proceeding. A few situations in which this may be necessary, but not limited to are mentioned below:

1. Any lawsuit involving the estate.
2. Disagreements among heirs.
3. IRS problems that involve the estate.

The material contained here is not intended to be a substitution for legal advice in any way, shape, or form. Instead, its intent is to inform and familiarize you with probate procedures so that you can intelligently be an integral part of the estate closing process for which you have been appointed to represent.

Whether it is your desire to be a "hands on" personal representative or you are simply seeking information to learn how your own estate might be administered, after reading the information contained here you will no doubt have a much better understanding of how the probate process works. Again, the information contained here should be used as a reference for administering non-complicated estates. Being an active participant in the estate closing process gives one the feeling of satisfaction and contentment knowing that they were a vital part of the administration of the estate they were appointed to represent. By knowing confidently firsthand that the wishes of your loved one have been carried out accurately and completely, you will experience a greater feeling of accomplishment. Oftentimes, just occupying yourself with all the different tasks involved in the process of closing the estate may help ease the grieving process.

Usually, most people would just find an attorney and collect all of the decedent's documents that they can find; such as, bills, insurance papers, mortgages, tax information, etc; place everything together in one large box, and turn everything over to the attorney to handle. Without knowing how the process works it can all seem very intimidating and overwhelming. It then becomes much easier and less stressful to simply turn everything over to your attorney to sift through. If it is your desire, however, you can do much more than just hold the title of executor, or personal representative. With proper organization, time, and perseverance you will close the estate of your loved one with pride, dignity, and an overwhelming feeling of accomplishment.

SECTION I

EASY ESTATE CLOSING TECHNIQUES

****

CHAPTER ONE

Is Probate Really Necessary?

What is a Will?

What if there is Not a Will?

How To Find the Right Attorney?

Is Probate Really Necessary?

Is probate really necessary? This is a good question. Surprisingly, in some cases probate is not necessary. For instance, if the decedent has a surviving spouse, ownership usually automatically transfers to the surviving spouse. In cases where assets were placed in a trust, usually things are handled according to the terms of the trust. For instance, if the decedent had a living trust, probate could then be avoided. The terms of the living trust must then be carried out, in accordance to its detailed instructions, and thus eliminating the need for probate. Also, if a decedent has limited assets below a certain dollar figure, probate may possibly be avoided. However, if there are wages, automobiles, bank accounts, real estate, it would be in the best interest of the estate to consult a probate attorney to determine if probate can be passed. You can also check the applicable provisions of the law in the state where the decedent resided. If there are assets that must be distributed to beneficiaries, without the involvement of any trusts, there is probably a good chance that it will need to be probated.

WHAT IS A WILL?

Before someone dies they have the option of writing a Will. This is a written, witnessed, notarized legal description of how you want your assets distributed. Essentially, a will is designed to act as legal instructions of what you want done with your personal property and assets.

Consult an attorney before writing a will to make sure it is a sound document and has all the necessary components to stand in a court of law.

WHAT IF THERE IS NOT A WILL?

If the decedent left no valid will, and has not appointed anyone to fill the position of his or her personal representative, a personal representative (called an administrator) is then appointed by the probate court in the county where the decedent resided. In situations where no will is present, this is referred to as a state of intestacy. Probate will most likely be done in the same state and county where the decedent lived. In most cases, the spouse or adult children will be named as the administrator of the estate by the probate court.

If the decedent did not name a personal representative, and if no persons with close relationships come to the court's attention, it is very likely that the court would then utilize its own discretion and possibly name someone totally unknown to the decedent and clueless to the decedent's affairs. This is done in some cases to avoid conflicts of interest. If for example, there were a brother and sister in line to be appointed as administrator, or co-administrator, if the court were to become aware of this the court could possibly appoint someone completely neutral and unbiased to handle the decedent's affairs in a manner so as to not favor one sibling over another sibling. This could, however, result in the wishes of the decedent not being carried out according to the desires of the decedent. In fact, this could greatly conflict with the actual wishes of the decedent.

How to find the Right Attorney?

If the decedent died intestate, meaning without a will, you have complete freedom to select an attorney for the administration of the estate. If the decedent died testate meaning with a valid will, you will usually still have the authority to change attorneys, even if the testator made their attorney choice known in his or her will. Under the law, in some states, this will probably be considered as simply a suggestion on the part of the testator, and therefore not binding. However, since the attorney will be a vital part of the estate administration, it is imperative that the personal representative select an individual who they can feel very comfortable working with most effectively. Regardless of the different types or amounts of assets in the estate, practically all cases will probably require the need for legal and tax professionals to ensure that these types of matters are handled correctly.

For instance, you would not want to hire an entertainment attorney to handle a malpractice issue. In the same likeness, you would not want to hire an adoption attorney to handle probate issues.

Be careful to select an attorney with absolute consideration of their experience with estate planning and probate issues.

Most attorneys that are experienced in estate law are knowledgeable and are very much aware of what procedures are necessary to ensure that document preparation and filing of those documents are done so in a timely manner. So, as to ensure, that no deadlines are missed.

Be certain, before any work begins, that reasonable fees have been agreed upon by all parties. The fee agreement should always be done in writing and signed by all parties.

Read it carefully. Make it a point to speak with at least two or three attorneys before hiring an attorney to assist you with the probate process. Select an attorney that is the most knowledgeable in this area of the law, and that you feel most comfortable working with.

Don't select someone simply because of lower fees. Look for an attorney that is knowledgeable and who has good experience, and expertise in estate planning and administration. These attorneys will spend less hours researching issues, which can equate to quite a savings for the estate by avoiding time consuming errors.

CHAPTER TWO

Executor   or Executrix ?

Co-Executors

What is a Trustee?

Executor or Executrix?

The title of the personal representative is determined by how they are selected or appointed. An executor is referred to as a male, while an executrix is known as a female. In some cases, a company or bank can be appointed to represent the estate. They too would be referred to as executors.

Co-Executors

In many cases more than one person can be selected to serve as personal representative for an estate. A husband can name his surviving spouse and another person or entity such as a bank as co-executors; if all the executors named in a will elect to function as such, there would be a serious need for all the parties to be able to work together to get the job accomplished.

Co-executors that are named in a will do not have to accept the appointment. If a person chooses to, they can decline from serving as a co-executor. This is not considered to be uncommon. This could occur in the case of the children of the decedent that are named as co-executors who live in another state and are not physically available to handle the affairs of the decedent. In some cases co-executors may be chosen because they each have some unique knowledge of the affairs of the decedent. For example, the decedent may choose to name a banker as co-executor as mentioned earlier. The banker may have specific knowledge of the decedent's personal and financial affairs.

What is a Trustee?

A trustee is a legal arrangement whereby the title to certain property is to be held by one party (which would be the trustee), who is legally responsible for using that property for the benefit of one or more other persons designated by the originator of the trust. These persons are referred to as the beneficiaries. Trustee appointments are usually made to handle affairs for minor children or individuals that are incompetent.

CHAPTER THREE

Selecting a Personal Representative

The Job Description of the Personal Representative

Becoming a Personal Representative

Selecting a Personal Representative

When writing a will it is important to name or appoint a responsible individual that you wish to oversee or to follow through with the instructions set forth in your will. In most cases you will refer to that individual as a Personal Representative or an Executor. We use the term 'personal representative' as our point of reference throughout this material.

It is a good idea to have a discussion with the individual(s) that you have selected so that those individuals have full knowledge of your desires, and so that your wishes are clear enough to be carried out correctly.

It is very common to also select and name an alternate personal representative to serve as a back up to your first choice. So that if for any reason your first choice can not perform the responsibilities set forth in your will, you will have someone ready to fill in. It may be the case that the selected party feels that altogether the risks, time involved, and multiple responsibilities are more than they wish to commit themselves to, and for these reasons alone may decide to decline serving as personal representative. Realizing that, unless they can be totally committed, it would probably not be in the best interest of the estate for them to serve. You must consider whether the person(s) you have chosen to represent your estate is capable of handling the many important tasks involved. A copy of your will should be given to the individual you have chosen to represent your estate, and to your attorney.

THE JOB DESCRIPTION OF THE PERSONAL REPRESENTATIVE

When a person dies, it becomes the responsibility of the personal representative to collect all of the decedent's personal property. You will need to make a list of all the creditors that are owed. List these creditors in alphabetical order. As you list the names of creditors, also include their phone number, address, and the balance owing, according to the most recent billing statements that you have collected. This is so that you have easy access to the creditor's phone number which will allow contact to be made more easily.

You will have the address handy in case you need to correspond with them or send a payment. You can do this after you have collected all of the credit statements belonging to the decedent.

After you have a list from which to work of all the creditors, place phone calls to each creditor immediately to close each account, and to verify the current balance owing. Be sure to check for any discrepancies. When you place calls to these creditors, be sure to ask to speak to the credit manager, supervisor or someone of an authoritative position of the company. Identify yourself as an officer of the decedent's estate with the title that you have been appointed.

Document all conversations between the creditors and yourself. Billing statements are not always accurate so it is important to get this information verified directly by the creditor. In addition to always documenting the name of the person that you speak with for a particular creditor, also document the nature of the conversation, and be sure to leave enough room for any future notes that are sure to take place throughout the estate closing process with that particular creditor. It may be necessary for you to provide documentation proving that you are truly the personal representative of the estate that you are claiming to represent, since much of the information that you will be requesting will be of a confidential nature. The document that will provide the proof that you need is called the *'Letters testamentary'* in some states (See Chapter Four, Probate Documents for further clarification). This is the document provided to you by the probate court formally appointing you as either the executor, or personal representative of the estate. With this document, you can now conduct business on behalf of the estate. After receiving the Letters Testamentary document from the probate court, you should contact the IRS immediately to request an SS4 tax application form. This application must be completed in order to receive a Tax ID number for the estate.

Upon receiving the Tax ID Number, you can now open a bank account on behalf of the estate. This bank account will include your name and title, as well as the estate name.

As soon as you have received checks from the bank, and you have received approval from the court, you can begin paying debts on behalf of the estate. You should at no time, under any circumstances commingle the funds of the estate with your own monies.

Develop a filing system that will work best for you. Below is a list of some files that will make getting organized easier. Create files that pertain to your particular circumstances and needs. Below are some examples:

1) Attorney Correspondence
2) Credit Accounts Unpaid
3) Credit Accounts Paid
4) Bank Statements
5) Health/Life Insurance Policies

6)   Investments

7)   Medical & Dental Accounts

8)   Real Estate Owned (Listing individual files for each property)

9)   Property Taxes

10)   Income Taxes

Make yourself a special notebook for the specific purpose of maintaining records as it pertains to pertinent information concerning each file. As previously suggested, you should record the date, time, balances owed and other pertinent information. You should keep documentation for everything associated with the estate.

After debt, taxes, and expenses are paid, and after you have received approval from the probate court, the remaining assets can be distributed to the decedent's beneficiaries. Distribution is determined by the person's Will, or the intestacy laws, which are laws that preside over the distribution of the estate if a person should die without a Will. It is the personal representative's responsibility to collect and distribute assets and to pay the death taxes and expenses of the decedent if applicable. Keep in mind that you could be liable for any errors or mistakes.

While most personal representatives may take their position seriously, and perform these tasks in an efficient manner, it does not always happen this way. State laws usually hold the personal representative to the same standard of care of a reasonable, efficient person operating in most normal circumstances. It's important to note that what is reasonable and efficient to you, as the personal representative, is not always reasonable and efficient to the beneficiaries. It is important to handle the affairs of the decedent with the same good judgment as you would with your own affairs.

If the court discovers that the personal representative has not performed in the best interest of the estate and the beneficiaries, the personal representative could be held accountable. This means, (as noted above), that the personal representative is personally liable for any errors or mistakes made while administrating the decedent's estate, and could be issued monetary penalties by the probate court.

BECOMING A PERSONAL REPRESENTATIVE

Let's visualize for a moment that the owner of a television production company selected you, his best friend to become personal representative of his estate. Say you have never done this before, and you know absolutely nothing about closing estates and even less about running the business that he owned. Furthermore, you have never managed a business before in your life, and you haven't a clue as to what lies ahead as far as what expectations await you in terms of what your obligations, duties, and responsibilities are, and precisely what legal issues that you need to be concerned about as you suddenly fall into this new position that appears to have just fallen from the sky into your lap.

In much the same way, as personal representative you are totally unaware of what is expected by those that would benefit from the estate, as well as what you should do where creditors are concerned. You are basically pretty much in the dark. What you need now is guidance through this process for the position that you have been appointed to uphold.

You will find that the process is much less intimidating than one might think. You simply need to develop a plan of action and work your plan in an organized manner.

In many cases, when a person dies without a will, and owns property that is worth any real value, the probate court will usually appoint someone to administer the estate. That person could be either one or several individuals. It could consist of a bank or trust company that acts on the behalf of the deceased. They too could be given the title of 'personal representative'. The duties, responsibilities and title of the personal representative may differ depending on the state laws where the decedent resides as well as what special circumstances may apply to your particular situation.

It is imperative that accurate record keeping be maintained, and regarded with the utmost importance as courts can require you, (the personal representative) to pay out of your own pocket for any errors, procedures that you failed to follow, or for being late with various court filings. So in essence, your lack of knowledge can make you become personally responsible and liable. This is why it's important to put together an estate advisor group. This group would consist of individuals that are knowledgeable in areas where experienced, informed advice is needed for a certain area of the estate. Such as, for tax returns you would hire a tax consultant. For information regarding stocks and bonds you would consult an investment broker. When true market values are needed, you would need to consult an appraiser. Use good judgment when utilizing the members of this group, keeping in mind that any decisions made will fall on your shoulders. Negotiate fees with them before they begin working for the estate. You will need the expertise of other professionals as well that specialize in specific areas of the estate that you are dealing with. Such as, real estate agents, insurance agents, etc. These may become necessary as your situation warrants. For example, before having an estate sale, hire an appraiser to appraise property before the sale. The advisors that you select will be dependent upon the specific situation in the estate you are handling.

Below is an example of how important the role of personal representative is:

Jon Gaviston was an art collector and antique dealer. He was a widower and had three young adult children that were attending various colleges some 2,000 miles away. He owned a magnificent home with a swimming pool, and tennis court. He even hired a personal staff that worked a few days a week to assist him with running his home. One day as he was climbing up his built-in staircase to recover some paintings from his attic, he missed a stair, lost his balance and fell to his death. Mr. Gaviston probably selected a personal representative that was knowledgeable about both his antique business and his art collection. His personal staff would need to be paid. Any unsatisfied loans that he may have secured in order to acquire some of his art or antiques would now need to be satisfied. By the same token, any outstanding money that was owed to him would now need to be collected. His outstanding bills would need to be paid. The sale of his beautiful home may possibly now need to be considered. Lots of important decisions would now have to be made. All of his assets would need to be collected. The instructions that Mr. Gaviston left in his will would now need to be carried out. Bank and credit accounts must now be closed by the personal representative that Mr. Gaviston selected. It would become the responsibility of the personal representative that Mr. Gaviston selected to carry out all of these duties.

CHAPTER FOUR

Time to Get Organized !

How to Conduct an Inventory & Organize Documents

Probate Documents

TIME TO GET ORGANIZED!

Basic, but good organizational skills are essential for the personal representative that is concerned with closing the estate properly. It is imperative that the person in charge of closing the estate, whether it is an executor or personal representative, be extremely organized. That will be the first step in closing an estate. You will be responsible for organizing and pulling together basically numerous documents and assets, which will include personal and financial data, as well as all personal property belonging to the decedent.

You will need a clean open space in which to work. Your kitchen table will suffice as your new work station. It will be necessary for you to have the following supplies to assist you with the organizational process:

1. Pens and pencils

2. Notebook Tablet & Note Paper

3. File Folders and Labels

4. Paperclips

5. Stapler/staples

6. Highlighters

7. Calculator

Organize your supplies so that they are all readily available as needed. Place pens, pencils, highlighters, stapler, staples, paperclips, and file labels in one large container with lid, or a large box.

Invest in a file cabinet that is suitable for storing the files that you will need to make. Once files are made, file them in alphabetical order for easy retrieval and access.

Remember, good organization is the key to your success in carrying out the many tasks involved in closing an estate.

HOW TO CONDUCT AN INVENTORY AND ORGANIZE DOCUMENTS

After getting organized, you will need to develop an inventory of all of the decedent's property. Locating and developing a list of all important documents will be your next priority. You will need these documents to determine assets, personal property, insurance information, debts that are owed by the decedent, investment information, real estate owned by the decedent, etc.

In a notebook, make a log of all of the decedent's personal possessions. If an estate sale is necessary, this list will help you to identify items.

Documents that you will need to locate should include current bank account statements, credit account statements, life and health insurance policies, fire liability and other insurance policies, property tax information, real estate deeds, wills and trusts, stocks and bonds, and other securities, birth certificates, marriage licenses, and marital agreements, military service records, social security information, and income tax information.

Make special files for each of the categories that you have documents for, as additional documents may also be collected under these same subject matters. In other words, it is very likely that additional paperwork pertaining to each of these categories will increase. You will need a safe, locked area in which to store these documents. As mentioned above, filing documents in alphabetical order will allow for easy access and retrieval.

PROBATE DOCUMENTS

Throughout the probate process it will become necessary for many different documents to be signed by you, and by your attorney on behalf of the estate which will subsequently be filed with the probate court. Some of the documents you possibly may use have been identified below. Following the name of the document is a brief description of what the particular document's purpose is.

Keep in mind, names of the documents mentioned here may differ from what they may be referred to in your area, however, the purpose may be the same.

1) <u>Death Certificate</u> – The death certificate will include pertinent information concerning the decedent's death. Such as personal information, as well as, time and cause of death. This document can be obtained from your local Health and Vital Statistics

Division. The death certificate will be stamped and dated with an official state seal by the state Registrar representing the local state health division that the decedent resided in. There is usually a nominal fee to obtain each original death certificate. You can make copies, however, in most cases, in order for you to conduct business on behalf of the estate, you will need to provide most businesses with an original death certificate. You may discover that you will need several original death certificates throughout the probate process.

Financial institutions, such as banks, insurance companies, investment companies, etc. will all most likely require that you provide them with original death certificates.

2) <u>Last Will and Testament & Codicils</u> – The Last Will and Testament is a document that outlines the personal instructions and the decedent's wishes. It also describes how the distribution of assets of the

decedent is to be accomplished. It holds all of the necessary information describing how the decedent's estate is to be distributed. It must be signed, dated, witnessed, (in some cases by two persons), and notarized in ordered for it to be recognized as legal and binding.

The advice of an attorney should be obtained to ensure that the will is legal and binding and will have no problem standing up in a court of law.

A <u>Codicil</u> is an addition to an existing Will and Testament. In other words, this is a way of adding more instructions without rewriting the entire will. If it is the case that there has been more than one codicil written by the decedent, the last codicil written may be the one that is actually used and followed. However, all of the codicils will be considered. You will need to seek the advice of an attorney in situations where there are multiple codicils.

3) <u>Letters Testamentary</u> – A legal document that comes from the probate court which formally appoints the Personal Representative or Executor as the legal representative of the estate. This document also certifies the will, and actually sets the wheels of probate into action. It gives you the authority to act as a legal representative of the estate.

4) <u>Inventory </u>– A complete estimated inventory of the estate in its entirety must be filed with the court. This inventory will include all assets belonging to the decedent. Within a certain time period after your appointment by the court, to be determined by the probate court in your state, (60 days in some states), you will be required to file an inventory of these assets with the court. Your attorney will use the information that you supply regarding all of the decedent's assets to compile an estimated inventory for the probate court.

This should be done by your attorney as critical time periods must be honored to avoid being served notice and possible penalties by the court.

5) <u>Public Notice</u> – A public notice must be placed in your local newspaper notifying all possible creditors of the decedent's death. This serves as a good faith effort to give all creditors the opportunity to file any claims against the estate to collect any outstanding debts owed by the decedent.

The notice should include your name, title and address, as well as the name and contact information of the attorney of record representing the estate.

6) <u>Search for Creditors</u> – In many cases, after public notice has been published it may be necessary for an affidavit of Compliance regarding the search for creditors to be filed with the court by your attorney to inform the court that the search has been completed.

7) <u>Final Accounting/Petition for Decree of Final Distribution</u> – This document will outline the accounting of the estate. It will include banking data, estate sales information, debt payments and tax information as well as asset distribution information. This document will show a full accounting of all of the estate activity. This will include financial and property within the estate, as well as how it all was distributed.

8) <u>Notice for Filing Objections to Final Account</u> This document must be sent to all heirs of the estate. This gives all of the heirs the opportunity to file any objections with the court before the distribution of any assets.

9) <u>Order Approving Final Account & Decree of Final Distribution</u> – After the final account has been filed with the probate court and the time for filing an objection has passed with no objections filed,

the Order Approving Final Accounting of the estate document can now be submitted to the probate court requesting final approval to distribute the remaining assets of the estate to the designated heirs.

10) <u>Order Discharging Executor or Personal Representative</u> – After all conditions of the will and the probate court have been met, the order discharging you as Personal Representative is to simply ask the court to relieve the Executor or Personal Representative from their duty and for the closing of the estate to be allowed.

The court documents filed on behalf of the estate throughout the probate process should be tailored to fit your particular circumstances.

They are, however, not limited to the documents listed above.

CHAPTER FIVE

Administration of the Estate - Overview

Personal Representative Fee for Services

Communicating with the Beneficiaries

How to Avoid Liability

About Tax Returns

ADMINISTRATION OF THE ESTATE -

Overview

As the personal representative or executor of an estate, you are now being considered as an officer of the court, as well as having a responsibility to the court for the accurate and proper administration of the estate. In some states, you may be required by law to obtain an attorney. You will need to check the laws in your particular area to see how this applies to your situation. Also, in some states, there are special rules that you must follow in closing estates.

At any rate, there are several things that you must do immediately to preserve and protect the interests of the estate and its beneficiaries. Following is an overview of probate procedures that may assist you with the estate closing process.

You will need to first obtain one to three original certified death certificates, depending on the amount of companies that require it. You may find that you will need more at a later time. Your attorney will need a true copy (original) death certificate, as well as a copy of the <u>Last Will and Testament and any codicils</u> that may exist. The attorney will then make a petition to the court for probate of the Will and Appointment of the Executor or Personal Representative of the estate. This procedure is how you are officially and legally named Executor or Personal Representative by the probate court.

The <u>Last Will and Testament</u> will be filed with the court along with the petition requesting probate. The court will at that time issue a file with a <u>Case Number</u>. The case number will be included on all future court documents. You can review the probate file by going to your county courthouse file room for probate cases, and giving the court clerk the case number, or file number, that you have been issued. In some states, as discussed earlier, you will be issued a legal document from the court called <u>Letters Testamentary</u>. This document shows clearly your appointment as the legal Executor or Personal Representative of the will. In some states, this document will be signed by the court administrator and stamped with a court seal. This document, as with all subsequent documents will display the court case number that has been assigned to your probate file.

The Letters Testamentary document is a very important document. It indicates that you have been appointed by the court to represent the estate. With this document you can now conduct business on behalf of the estate. It will be necessary to produce this document with photo identification when dealing with certain businesses such as banks, and other financial institutions.

Once you have this form, you will need to contact the IRS to request a SS4 form, which is a Tax Application form for the issuance of a Tax Identification number. A tax identification number is needed to open a separate bank account on behalf of the estate. This is necessary because all monies involving the estate must be kept separate from any other person's assets, and monies. No loans are to be made on behalf of the estate without prior permission of the court.

In some states, within sixty days of being appointed by the court you are required to file an <u>Inventory</u> of the estate to the court. The inventory is the document that describes the estimated cash value of the estate. Any real property owned along with their estimated cash values would be reported on this document. Also, the estimated cash value of all personal property owned would be included on this document. The inventory is very important in that if not submitted to the court within the specified time frame which is designated by the probate court, you could receive notice or even penalties by the probate court.

In order to adequately administer the estate, after receiving the Tax ID number open a checking account for the estate. All monies involving the estate should flow through this estate checking account. This establishes a permanent record that can be accurately verified by the banks' records.

Many banks will set up a separate checking account for the estate identifying you as the Personal Representative, Executor, etc, on the check. Before setting up the bank account speak to a few bankers. Choose the bank that offers the best services at the lowest cost. Select an interest bearing account. Always keep a record of all transactions. Keep all receipts. Itemize in detail an explanation for each check written.

All bills that are paid, including medical bills, should be recorded. Any bills that are paid should be paid through this account. At no time should any monies from the estate be commingled with the personal monies of the estate representative.

The post office should be notified immediately of where to send the decedent's mail. Notify everyone that had contact with the decedent. Notify creditors. You must advertise your appointment and notice of the death of the decedent in your local newspaper. Your attorney can assist you with this, as there are time requirements that must be honored.

Jewelry should be immediately collected and placed in a safe deposit box. An appraisal should be completed to determine the value of various items such as jewelry, furniture, dishes, etc.

Once you have been granted permission to do so, any bills owed by the decedent should be paid from the checking account opened on behalf of the estate. It is essential that you obtain a receipt for all bills that are paid on behalf of the estate. These receipts will be needed later when submitting the final accounting.

Some important tips to remember are listed as follows:

If the decedent specifically leaves an article to a beneficiary (also known as bequeaths), that article should be distributed to that individual after being inventoried and appraised. If the item was not bequeathed to a beneficiary and monies are needed to pay taxes, or bills, the items can be sold after being inventoried and appraised. Estate sales should be put in motion as soon as possible to avoid any loss of value of the article. Do not purchase any of the articles yourself if a conflict of interest could arise from it to avoid court action that could be taken against you.

Group Life Insurance – Claims may need to be filed with work related insurance companies of the decedent. These claims are usually paid directly to the beneficiaries after an original death certificate and claim form is submitted with the appropriate information to the insurance company.

Life Insurance – If it has been so designated that life insurance is to be paid directly to the beneficiaries, or to the estate you should simply contact the agent or company and ask them what is needed to file a claim. Make sure to photo copy the entire policy before sending it in to the insurance company. Insurance companies usually require an original copy of the death certificate. Life insurance policies are usually paid in accordance to the instructions given by the decedent. Claims are usually paid directly to the beneficiaries.

Cash - Any cash found belonging to the decedent should be recorded and placed in a safe deposit box for safekeeping. It should later be deposited into the estate bank account.

PERSONAL REPRESENTATIVE
FEE FOR SERVICES

Questions may come up pertaining to how much money a personal representative should be paid for the services he or she will perform. Personal representatives are entitled to a fee in accordance with state laws. A good place to check is the statutory law of the state where the estate is being probated. Some states already have some standard fixed fees already in place. Any probate attorney should also be knowledgeable of the fee structure available to the personal representative. It is customary for the personal representative to receive reasonable compensation for services. If a personal representative spends hundreds of hours performing their duties, compensation for services should match the time and quality of the work performed.

The personal representative should keep a detailed log of how much time was spent doing which tasks, as well as information regarding expenses that were paid in the interest of the estate. It is a good idea for the Personal Representative to also make periodic progress reports to the beneficiaries, as well as submit bills for services rendered from time to time, so that the beneficiaries have a clear understanding of what is being done, and at what cost. This also eliminates the element of surprise on the part of the beneficiaries as to what the personal representative is charging for services which will result in smoother relations between the personal representative and the beneficiaries.

Always, before any work has started, negotiate and settle all fee concerning agreements in writing trying to base your understanding on how complex certain issues are intended to be. Many beneficiaries have already figured out what they plan to do with their financial portions before they ever receive their shares. Learning at the last minute that the personal representative expects to receive a large portion of the money for services performed that they were completely unaware of will be met with some very unhappy beneficiaries, (and that's putting it mildly), who just may contest this in court. In the case where there are more than one personal representative or executor, fees are usually divided equally.

COMMUNICATING WITH BENEFICIARIES

It is important to keep beneficiaries informed and to keep written notes of your conversations with those individuals. Your notes should consist of the date and time that you spoke, as well as the content of the conversation.

HOW TO AVOID LIABILITY

Your first duty as a personal representative to the family of the decedent should be loyalty and confidentiality. It is unprofessional to discuss details about the estate or its affairs with individuals not directly connected to the estate. Avoid situations that could be construed as a conflict of interest. Do not place yourself in a compromising situation where your interests are placed above the interests of those you have been entrusted to represent. With exception to the fee for the services you are performing, providing you have not agreed to work without a fee, and if the will does not specifically cancel out any such fee, you are not to gain any personal benefit from, or receive any extra monetary benefit while working for the estate.

As a legal or estate representative, you have an obligation to demonstrate the utmost care, professionalism, and efficiency while handling the estate's affairs. Your actions will most likely be considered reasonable and professional if you conduct yourself, and the business affairs of the estate with the same care, commitment and respect that you would in taking care of your own personal business activities. It is highly likely that you could get fined or end up with lawsuits if you fail to exercise true efficiency, and professionalism to do all that is necessary to safely guard the estate, it's assets, and beneficiaries. You must also make sure that you attempt to generate additional growth when applicable for the estate.

If you intentionally violate or fail to perform the duties expected of you as personal representative, and your actions result in a loss to the estate or it's beneficiaries, you could be considered negligent and you could become liable for damages. A beneficiary can recover whatever value that he/she would have had if there had not been the negligent act on the part of the personal representative that was representing the estate. If you sell assets or property without obtaining proper authorization and in that process the beneficiaries lose their interest, if you recklessly spend monies, or if you exercise clear conflicts of interests; such as, giving property of the estate to friends or family of your own, you could be sued and would very likely be held liable for damages. Seek legal professional advice before taking any action, such as described above.

When all of the conditions of the probate court have been met, and the proper approval has been received by the probate court to distribute assets to beneficiaries, for your protection, take the following steps:

1) Obtain a receipt for any assets you distribute to a beneficiary. The receipt should be a detailed description of the asset. This is done in order for you to be able to prove what was distributed, to whom, and when. It should also show that the beneficiary

has accepted the asset from the estate, by way of a signature. If he has signed a receipt in full for his share, he then must prove that he did not receive everything that he was expected to receive according to the will instructions.

2) Obtain written consent of all beneficiaries who are of legal age before modifying or making any investments.

3) Obtain a release stating that you are to be discharged from any liability of past actions.

4) Request a court order to be discharged as personal representative from probate court. The court order is to authorize your release as personal representative. This action will protect you from any future liability. This is usually done after the court has received an accounting of the estate. You must account for everything that was done during the administration of the estate. This includes providing

for the court cancelled checks, receipts, bills, to whom assets were distributed to, and when. This will show that you have properly carried out the terms of the will in its entirety.

ABOUT TAX RETURNS

Since an estate is considered to be a taxable entity, just like an individual person, during the administration of the estate, if the estate exceeds $600 you are required to file an IRS return for the estate. The estate will be considered a tax payer until the assets in the estate have been distributed, and there is nothing left to distribute.

The estate will be issued its own identification number, known as the Tax ID Number, or Employer Identification Number. You will use this number on all of your tax forms for the estate. You can obtain this number by contacting the IRS directly to request IRS form SS4. This should be taken care of soon after your personal representative appointment.

Certain taxes may apply to your situation such as death tax, inheritance tax, estate tax, and property transfer taxes so be sure to consult a probate attorney or tax consultant regarding these or any other tax related issues. Remember, it is the responsibility of the personal representative to be aware of the appropriate filing dates and to be certain that accurate returns are filed on behalf of the estate by the deadline of April 15 of the year following the decedent's death. It is also the responsibility of the personal representative to see that taxes are paid by that same date. If more time is needed to prepare the estate taxes, an extension can be filed through the IRS by completing the necessary forms.

Consult the advice of a tax professional when filing tax returns.

SECTION II

NEW STRATEGIES FOR PRE-DEATH PLANNING

****

NEW STRATGIES FOR PRE-DEATH PLANNING

Let's face it, none of us are looking forward to any sudden out-of-the-blue health challenges, such as becoming terminally ill. However, sometimes things happen that are out of our control, and with a little pre-planning you can have peace knowing that you have taken the few necessary steps to protect both your assets, and your beneficiaries. Your time will be free to concentrate solely on the medical challenge that you are facing.

Having to worry about everything at once such as: your assets, how your estate should bc handled should something happen to you, whether your loved ones will receive the benefits that you desire them to have; all of these worries combined with the medical crisis that you are facing can be extremely overwhelming, and will probably trigger additional stress. By alleviating this burden, you are allowing yourself the freedom to deal solely with your health condition without the additional stress of worrying about estate issues.

By planning ahead, the task of administering your estate will become much easier to be accomplished by the personal representative that you have selected. While making the administration of your estate easier, you can at the same time create additional cash flow for the beneficiaries of your estate. To accomplish this, consider exercising the simple strategies below:

1) Making the administration of the estate easier.

2) Increase the value of the estate that the beneficiaries would receive.

3) Reduce the costs of transfers.

4) Reduce income taxes.

5) Increase cash flow to pay taxes, and other expenses.

Taking the right approach basically anytime before death could make the job of the personal representative so much easier and at the same time could increase the monetary gain that the beneficiary is to receive greatly.

Let's take a closer look at each of the strategies mentioned above:

<u>Easier Administration of the Estate</u> – Prepare a clear and concise power of attorney. First thing to do is to have a trusted friend or relative sign a durable power of attorney.

A Power of Attorney is a legal document that authorizes you (or whomever it identifies) to represent the dying individual. The power of Attorney should indicate that the power given will carry over even if the dying person becomes incompetent, or if they should die. This way, the designated person would be able to sign any important documents, such as tax returns, legal forms, etc. and can act on your behalf in most all matters.

How to Increase the Value of the Estate – There are several ways that this can be accomplished. You can research insurance policies for what is known as a "waiver of premium". The ***waiver of premium*** clause requires the insurer to keep the policy in full force even if the insured should become disabled. In this case the policy holder does not have to worry about having to pay for premiums if they should become disabled. In some cases, the insurer will be required to repay back to the insured all premiums that were paid from the time of being disabled. This strategy would allow extra cash to go to your estate instead of insurance premiums, or it could be used to simply cover other costs that arise, such as housing, nursing home or medical costs. The policy cash values should continue to increase as if the insured was still paying premiums.

How to Reduce Transfer Costs – The cost of transferring property from one individual to another can be less costly by following these simple suggestions:

1) Update the Will – When was the last time that the will was updated? Make sure the will is current and has been recently updated. Current or recent laws may offer even greater savings. Discuss your situation with a tax advisor.

2) Repay any outstanding Life Insurance Policy Loans – If any loans against life insurance are repaid, the total cash value will then go to the beneficiaries. Life insurance policies are paid directly without having to go through the probate process. Life insurance is passed to its beneficiaries without being subjected to fees of any kind.

3) Be careful to not name the estate as the policy beneficiary. If you have named your estate as beneficiary of a life insurance policy (or if the beneficiary that you have previously named has predeceased you) then you should change your beneficiary as soon as possible to insure that it does not get claimed by taxes and creditors.

How to Lower your Income Taxes - Less taxes will mean more money for your beneficiaries.

a. Charitable Gifts – If you plan to give gifts in your will, you might want to consider giving any such gifts before your death. In most instances, the gift you give after death will be taxed. Therefore, that's money that could be saved if gifts are given before death.

b. Annual Federal Gift-Tax Exclusion – Each person is allowed to give up to $11,000 per year, in cash or property. After doing so, this amount can come off of your taxable income. What's great about this is that you may give to whomever you wish, whether it's a relative or not. Once the gift is made, it is removed from the estate. These gifts will escape probate and are therefore, not subject to possible will contest, taxes or fees. The power of attorney that you have selected is also authorized to pass these gifts on your behalf.

3. Maximize Benefits by utilizing New Tax Laws – Consult a tax advisor to ensure that your assets are set up in such a way that your family can receive all of the benefits that are available involving gift tax exemptions.

How to Create Cash to Pay Taxes and Other Expenses – You may want to consider an extended term insurance policy. However, some policies do not contain a waiver of premium notice. If this is the case, determine if your insurance company can convert the whole life policy to a term policy. This will allow you to not be required to make regular premiums, and you would receive coverage for a specified time period or term.

How to Make a List of Advisors – Names and addresses, phone numbers of bankers, insurance agents, brokers, accountants, attorneys and other advisors should also be placed in a safe deposit box and given to the personal representative that you have selected. Make sure the list of advisors is included in your Letter of Instructions as well.

Updating Key Documents – It is a good idea to review and change all wills, life insurance policies, and any other such important documents so that they remain current with all of the current beneficiary information being duly noted.

How to write a Letter of Instructions – A letter of instructions will be a personal, informal, handwritten or typed document usually left with either a very close friend or a trusted relative. This informal letter will explain your desires that you might consider too personal to become public information. So for this reason, instead of placing these particular instructions in your will, you will write out (separate from your will) any personal issues that you would like to have covered. This letter will describe urgent matters that you wish to be handled immediately following your death. This letter should also include a copy of your list of advisors so that they can be contacted for assistance. This will allow a smooth transition into the probate process and will help closing your estate to take place as smoothly as possible. Any person that you wish your personal representative to seek assistance or advice from should be included in the letter of instructions.

<u>Designating Domicile</u> – Designating domicile or residency will allow you to avoid being charged a death tax by more than one state. If the decedent lived in two or more houses, in various states in one year, it is possible that more than one state may attempt to tax their property unless their primary residence has been clearly established. There are a few things that must be done to accomplish this. The following strategies will assist you.

1) Register to vote in the chosen state.

2) Check to see if the chosen state has a certificate application to establish domicile (or residency) in that state.

3) Open both savings and checking bank accounts.

4) Be able to show mail addressed to you in the chosen state from credit card companies.

5) Obtain a driver's license in the chosen state.

6) Be able to produce social security correspondence, checks, etc. mailed to this location.

7) File tax returns from this location.

8) You must be able to show residency in the chosen state for at least six months.

HOW TO REDUCE FEES

Before you actually hire an attorney, ask for a written statement of their hourly fee and a rough estimate of the hours it will take to do the job. If you, in your position as Person Representative will be contacting creditors, paying bills, preparing sales of property (if necessary to pay bills), managing real estate property, etc. by all means, negotiate the fees. Approach the attorney from the standpoint of one professional to another. Negotiate an hourly rate as opposed to a large flat fee since you will be doing a great deal of the leg work.

SECTION III

DEALING WITH REAL ESTATE ISSUES

****

DEALING WITH REAL ESTATE ISSUES

Rented property – If the decedent was renting at the time of death, after reading over the rental agreement contract, you can then determine whether the estate has any further obligations due to the landlord.

If the decedent owned property it is important to determine what interest the decedent had in the property. You can do this by obtaining copies of the deeds and other evidence of title.

Make sure that the property is properly insured and that the insurance premiums are kept current. Pay monthly utilities to keep the lights and electricity on. You must maintain the premises in general.

If the property is rented you must notify the tenants in writing that you are the personal representative for the decedent's estate and advise the tenants of where they should now send all future rents to. All future rents should be deposited into the estate checking account. If plans are being made to sell that property the tenant should be advised.

Make sure that property taxes are paid and remain current.

Hire a Realtor if your objective is to sell the property. If it has not been bequeathed to anyone and this is the desire of the decedent, or the beneficiaries, or in the case where medical bills must be paid and you must generate money. However, state laws vary regarding the Personal Representative's right to sale real estate. Consult an attorney before you decide to sell. The following procedure may assist you with the sale of real estate:

1) Have the property appraised by a licensed real estate appraiser to determine the fair market value.

2) If you have not already been instructed by the decedent (in the will), obtain written permission from the beneficiaries to sell the property at an agreed upon price.

3) Have the procedure reviewed by legal counsel before signing any real estate documents unless you are familiar with real estate transactions.

Certain taxes may apply to your situation such as state death tax, inheritance tax, estate tax, and property transfers tax, consult a probate attorney or tax consultant regarding these issues.

GLOSSARY

<u>Accounting</u> – Financial records that are prepared for the court, the beneficiaries, and any other concerned person that is involved with the estate that clearly shows all transactions that have occurred from the beginning to the end of probate.

<u>Administration</u> – The management process of the estate for the decedent. It includes collecting all assets (both financial and physical), paying all debts and taxes owed, meeting probate court deadlines, and making distribution to the beneficiaries of the estate.

<u>Administrator</u> – The person appointed by the court to manage the estate if the deceased person did not

have a valid will; or if the will did not list an executor or personal representative.

Beneficiary – A person named in a will to inherit a part or share of the deceased person's estate. Also, a person named to receive an interest of a trust or insurance policy.

Bequest – A gift of property by a will. If a specific bequest is described in a will, usually reference is being made to some type of property (such as a house, a television set, or a coin collection).

Codicil – An addition to an existing will that adds, or modifies it. In order for a codicil to be executed it must be deemed valid in the same way that a will must be.

Decedent – A person that has died, male or female.

Disclaimer – When any bequeathed property is refused, and not accepted by the beneficiary.

Distribution – Personal property that is passed to the heirs of one who dies without having a will, as well as the passing of assets to the beneficiaries by the personal representative when a will is present.

Domicile – What is considered to be a person's permanent residence.

Executor – The individual selected, named and designated by the deceased in his or her will to manage the decedent's estate. This individual will act on behalf of the deceased person while handling all of the deceased person's affairs. This person is also known as the personal representative.

Fair Market Value –The current cost or value of any given property of the estate at the time of possible sale.

Fiduciary – One that is in a position of trust. Administrators, executors, guardians, personal representatives, and trustees all stand in a fiduciary relationship to persons whose personal, business, and legal affairs they are taking care of.

Heir - A person who has been named to receive an interest from the deceased person's estate.

Incompetent – A person who has been deemed legally unable to handle their own affairs.

Inheritance Tax – A tax placed on the heirs that is determined by the amount of the share that the beneficiary received.

Intangible Property – Property that is not of a physical nature, such as a watch or a ring. Only the item is evidence of its value, such as stocks and bonds, banking certificates, etc.

Intestate – Absent a will. A person that died without having a will is referred to has having died intestate.

Inventory – A record of the assets of an estate, that is compiled by the personal representative or attorney. This is usually required by the court and must be presented to the court within a certain timeframe towards the beginning of the probate process.

Irrevocable Trust – This type of trust cannot be revoked or terminated by the grantor. There are certain tax benefits that come along with this type of trust, so for this reason the grantor must give up all rights to alter, change, revoke or terminate the trust.

There are certain provisions that will allow this type of trust to be revoked, however it would involve the consent of the person that trust is for.

Power of Attorney – A written document that permits someone to name an individual to act on their behalf, should they become disabled or incapacitated. A power of attorney can sign documents, transfer property, and make important decisions for the incapacitated person.

Probate – The process of determining whether or not a will is valid as well as the execution of its content under the rules and guidance of the court.

Probate Property – Property that is passed in accordance to the will or probate laws.

Renunciation – An absolute refusal to accept one's interest, or property from the estate. When an individual totally gives up their right to receive property, and interest from the estate.

Revocable Trust – This type of trust can be changed or terminated at anytime during the grantor's lifetime, and whereby, the property in the trust can be taken back by the grantor if they should choose to do so.

Tangible Property – Tangible property is property that we can touch or see. Such as, automobiles, jewelry, clothes, furniture, etc.

Testamentary – By a will. A testamentary document is what is used to pass property and belongings at death, usually being in the form of a will.

Testate – When a will has been left to dispose of an individual's estate. The opposite of intestate.

Testator – The person who has a current will at the time of death.

Trust – A legal arrangement where property is held and managed by either an individual or an institution for the benefit of another person. Trustee – One that is entitled to legally hold property for the later use and benefit of another person.

Vested Interest – A stated interest in real or personal property.

Will – A document that describes your desires of what is to happen to your personal property, and assets, upon your death. In some states it is required that a will contain the signatures of two witnesses. However, the requirements may vary from state to state.

ABOUT THE AUTHOR

The author is an entrepreneur, freelance writer, wife and mother. She is a graduate of the Detroit Business Institute. She now lives in the Pacific Northwest with her family.

She has worked for several years in the Judicial Department as a judicial assistant to a district and circuit court judge. Her hobbies include reading, writing, and interior decorating.